Income Redistribution
and the Realignment
of American Politics

Income Redistribution and the Realignment of American Politics

Nolan M. McCarty,
Keith T. Poole, and
Howard Rosenthal

The AEI Press

Publisher for the American Enterprise Institute
WASHINGTON, D.C.

1997

We thank participants in panels at the Public Choice Society, the Midwest Political Science Association, and the Strategy and Politics Conference at the University of Maryland and participants in a seminar at Harvard University for comments.

Available in the United States from the AEI Press, c/o Publisher Resources Inc., 1224 Heil Quaker Blvd., P.O. Box 7001, La Vergne, TN 37086-7001. Distributed outside the United States by arrangement with Eurospan, 3 Henrietta Street, London WC2E 8LU England.

ISBN 0-8447-7078-7

1 3 5 7 9 10 8 6 4 2

The AEI PRESS
Publisher for the American Enterprise Institute
1150 17th Street, N.W., Washington, D.C. 20036

Printed in the United States of America

Contents

Foreword

This study is one of a series commissioned by the American Enterprise Institute on trends in the level and distribution of U.S. wages, income, wealth, consumption, and other measures of material welfare. The issues addressed in the series involve much more than dry statistics: they touch on fundamental aspirations of the American people—material progress, widely shared prosperity, and just reward for individual effort—and affect popular understanding of the successes and shortcomings of the private market economy and of particular government policies. For these reasons, discussions of "economic inequality" in the media and political debate are often partial and partisan as well as superficial. The AEI series is intended to improve the public discussion by bringing new data to light, exploring the strengths and weaknesses of various measures of economic welfare, and highlighting important questions of interpretations, causation, and consequence.

Each study in the series is presented and discussed in draft form at an AEI seminar prior to publication by the AEI Press. Marvin Kosters, director of economic policy studies at AEI, organized the series and moderated the seminars. A current list of published studies appears on the last page.

CHRISTOPHER DEMUTH
President, American Enterprise Institute

1

Introduction

Since the mid-1970s, American politics has become increasingly polarized around a left-right conflict along party lines. This conflict is basically over income redistribution. Other dimensions of conflict, particularly race, have largely vanished as distinct lines of conflict because they have been incorporated into left-right or liberal-conservative conflict. These changes are reflected in the slow disintegration of the southern Democratic Party, which began with the Goldwater presidential candidacy of 1964. The main pieces of evidence are as follows:

- Roll-call voting in Congress can increasingly be explained in terms of a one-dimensional, liberal-conservative conflict. While voting in the 104th House splits more frequently along a single dimension than at any time since the early years of this century, the present trend predates not only Newt Gingrich but also Ronald Reagan: the rise in unidimensionality began under Jimmy Carter. Although all roll calls are not strictly party-line votes, they increasingly divide just one of the two parties. In contrast, in the period from 1945 through 1976, most roll calls internally divided both parties.
- The overlap between the parties on the liberal-con-

1

servative dimension has been virtually eliminated. Moderates in both parties, particularly Republicans, have vanished. The distribution of members of Congress on the dimension has become increasingly bimodal. The distance separating the average Democrat from the average Republican has increased in time.

• The number of voters at least weakly identifying with one of the two parties has remained relatively constant since the end of World War II. This stability masks a dramatic shift of voters in the South from the Democratic Party to the Republican Party.

• Party identification has become more closely linked to income, with the Republicans becoming a party of the better off; the Democrats, the poor.

• As other issues have merged with income characteristics, African-American Democrats (both northern and southern) have come to anchor the left of the political spectrum in the House. Similarly, women in both parties are to the left of males. The redistributive effects of ending discrimination in the work place, affirmative action, welfare, child care, and food stamps appeal to women. The fact that women are more favorable to redistribution than men would be one explanation for the well-known gender gap in mass voting. The gender gap in Congress, however, does not persist once the characteristics of congressional districts are taken into account. Women are more liberal than men because they are elected from districts that support relatively liberal representatives. The same is not true for race. African-American representatives are more liberal even after controlling for the percentage of the population that is African-American and other characteristics of the congressional district. That is, the race gap in Congress echoes that in the mass public. The race gap, however, does not generate a distinct position. Since African-American Democrats are at the left end of the dimension, they tend to support all positions supported by moderately liberal white Democrats and, in addition, support even more liberal positions that attract a smaller number of white representatives.

• Consistent with the view that poor-rich divisions are increasingly defining liberal-conservative positions, "limousine liberal" representation has declined. In the 1970s, controlling for party, income was strongly negatively related to liberalism within the Democratic Party. "Limousine liberal" districts tended to anchor the left end of the liberal-conservative dimension. By 1996, however, this effect had decreased considerably in magnitude.

• Voting in presidential elections is increasingly linked to liberalism or conservatism and to income.

• The old Solid South has disappeared. The Republicans are now as well represented in the South as the Democrats at the presidential, congressional, and gubernatorial levels. While the Republican share of seats in southern state legislatures lags behind the party's gains at other levels, the Republican Party has dramatically increased its share of seats in the past twenty-five years.

• Changes in the South, in large part induced by the civil rights legislation of the 1960s, can explain much of the change but cannot explain the disappearance of moderation, as casually evidenced in the current confrontation between the legislative and the executive branches. Fortuitous events may have allowed the Democrats to promote redistributive, expensive programs that have brought about a polarizing backlash. One such event was the landslide victory handed the Democrats in 1964 by the candidacy of Barry Goldwater. Another was the disabling of the executive branch by Watergate after the 1972 elections, particularly following the midterm election of 1974.

In the remainder of the volume, we document these points, except for the last one, which is conjecture.

Our description of congressional ideology is largely based on our NOMINATE procedure (Poole and Rosenthal 1991, 1997), which uses all the roll calls cast by legislators over their careers to produce fine-grained measures of what is commonly referred to as *liberal-conservatism*. That is, it is widely accepted that Ted Kennedy and Ron Dellums are liberals, that Dick Armey and Jesse Helms are conservatives, and that Arlen Specter and Lee Hamilton are moderates. NOMINATE computes for each member of Congress a precise measure of liberalism or conservatism. Since NOMINATE uses all the roll calls cast by a member, the measure is more precise and less biased than the ratings published by such interest groups as the Americans for Democratic Action and the Americans for Constitutional Action.

Note that such expressions as *liberal, moderate,* and *conservative* are part of the common language not only of the players inside the Washington Beltway (politicians and the press) but also of many ordinary citizens. These terms are used to denote the political orientation of a member of Congress. Such labels are useful because they quickly furnish a rough guide to the positions a politician is likely to take on a wide variety of issues. For example, in contemporary politics, someone who favors a higher minimum wage is also likely to favor lower defense spending, favor affirmative action programs, oppose a balanced budget amendment to the Constitution, oppose lowering capital gains taxes, favor a no-striker-replacement law, oppose ending the entitlement status of welfare, and so on (in other words, a liberal Democrat). Indeed, this interrelationship between issues is so strong that just knowing that a politician opposes increasing the minimum wage is enough information to predict, with a fair degree of reliability, the politician's views on many seemingly unrelated issues.

This consistency or constraint (Converse 1964) of political opinions suggests that a politician's positions on a wide range of issues can be summarized by a simple formal structure. NOMINATE fits such a simple structure—a spatial or geometric model—to roll-call voting in Congress. Each legislator is represented by a point. (If the model has one dimension, the points are points on a line; two dimensions, points on a plane; three dimensions, points in a solid, etc.) Each roll call is represented by two points that correspond to the policy consequences of the yea and nay outcomes. The spatial model holds that a legislator prefers the closer of the two alternatives. The extent of preference is expressed by a utility function. The closer an alternative is to the legislator's ideal point, the greater the preference for the alternative and the higher the utility.

Through most of American history, two dimensions account for between 85 and 90 percent of roll-call voting decisions. The primary dimension almost always divides the two major parties, and the second dimension picks up regional divisions within the two major parties. In most periods, the first dimension is picking up, roughly speaking, the conflict between rich and poor, and the second dimension is based on race, North versus South.

We have scaled all roll-call votes from 1947 through 1995, using a dynamic version of NOMINATE (Poole and Rosenthal 1997, appendix A). This new procedure, DW-NOMINATE, is very similar to our earlier D-NOMINATE procedure (Poole and Rosenthal 1991).[1] The technical details of DW-NOMINATE are explained in appendix A to this volume.

The DW-NOMINATE estimation covers 1947–1995. The earlier D-NOMINATE estimation covered 1789–1985. In the overlapping years, 1947–1985, the two sets of estimates are essentially the same. In the postwar period, legislator positions are remarkably stable. Dramatic change—like that produced by the 1964 and the 1994 congressional elections—occurs mainly by replacement of legislators, not by conversions of individual legislators that disturb relative voting alignments. Stated in Darwinian terms, selection is far more important than adaptation.[2]

2

Unidimensionality

The basic change to unidimensionality is shown in figures 2–1, 2–2, 2–3, and 2–4. Figures 2–1 and 2–2 show the percentage of correct classifications from DW-NOMINATE for the House of Representatives (the figure for the Senate is similar). Figure 2–1 shows that the percentage of roll-call voting decisions classified by the first dimension begins to increase in the mid-1970s. The 104th Congress is the best-fitting since the early years of this century. In fact, the one-dimensional fit is now higher than any two-dimensional fit for all other postwar Congresses. The second dimension, which was improving classification by over 5 percent in the late 1950s, is now inconsequential.

As a result of unidimensionality, fewer and fewer roll calls divide both parties internally. Consider roll calls where the winning percentage was less than sixty. Figures 2–3 and 2–4 show the percentage of these close roll calls where more than 10 percent of each party disagreed with the majority of their respective party. The pattern in the two chambers is very similar; both show a very large drop since the mid-1970s.

It is important to note that the 104th House is but the continuation of increasing unidimensionality that began about 1973. Such an increase is thus the outgrowth

FIGURE 2–1
PERCENTAGE OF ROLL-CALL VOTES IN THE HOUSE OF REPRESENTATIVES CORRECTLY CLASSIFIED, 1947–1995

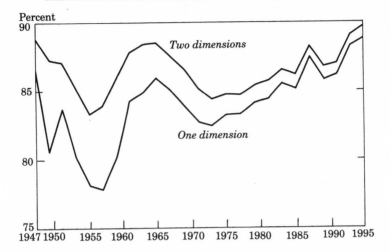

NOTE: Each plotted point represents one Congress.
SOURCE: Computations based on data from ICPSR for the 80th to the 101st Congresses (1947–1990). Data for the 102nd through the 104th Congresses (1991–1995) compiled by the authors.

of long-term changes in the substance of American politics rather than the shift in partisan control of Congress or changes in congressional rules and agenda selection effects.

Figures 2–5 and 2–6 show the distribution of legislators and roll-call cutting points (the point that divides those predicted on the liberal side of a roll call from those on the conservative side) in the 104th House for 1995. The Republican majority has used its agenda-setting powers to place most votes where they would internally divide the Democratic Party and capture the support of Democratic moderates, largely white male southern Democrats. Thus, most votes are not party-line votes. Moreover, the smooth, if sharply unimodal, distribution of cutting lines demonstrates that the spatial model of

FIGURE 2–2

PERCENTAGE GAIN IN ACCURACY OF CLASSIFYING ROLL-CALL
VOTES IN THE HOUSE OF REPRESENTATIVES FROM USING A TWO-
DIMENSIONAL SPATIAL MODEL, 1947–1995

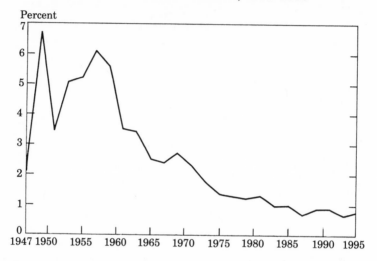

NOTE: Each plotted point represents one Congress.
SOURCE: Computations based on data from ICPSR for the 80th to
the 101st Congresses (1947–1990). Data for the 102nd through the
104th Congresses (1991–1995) compiled by the authors.

voting, with a continuum of liberal-conservative ideal
points, accounts for substantial behavior that cannot be
accounted for by a model of party discipline. This point is
illustrated by figure 2–7, which shows a histogram of the
twenty-three Republican defectors who (as of April 30,
1996) support increasing the minimum wage. The defectors are concentrated in the left tail of the Republican
Party.

FIGURE 2–3
PERCENTAGE OF CLOSE VOTES DIVIDING BOTH DEMOCRATS AND REPUBLICANS IN THE HOUSE OF REPRESENTATIVES, 1947–1995

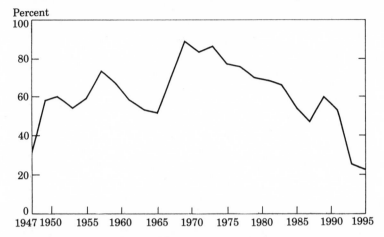

NOTE: Each plotted point represents one Congress.
SOURCE: Computations based on data from ICPSR for the 80th to the 101st Congresses (1947–1990). Data for the 102nd through the 104th Congresses (1991–1995) compiled by the authors.

FIGURE 2–4
PERCENTAGE OF CLOSE VOTES DIVIDING BOTH DEMOCRATS AND
REPUBLICANS IN THE SENATE, 1947–1995

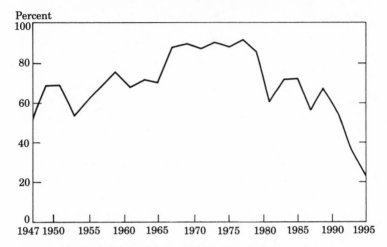

NOTE: Each plotted point represents one Congress.
SOURCE: Computations based on data from ICPSR for the 80th to
the 101st Congresses (1947–1990). Data for the 102nd through the
104th Congresses (1991–1995) compiled by the authors.

FIGURE 2–5
DISTRIBUTION OF LEGISLATORS IN THE 104TH HOUSE OF REPRESENTATIVES, 1995

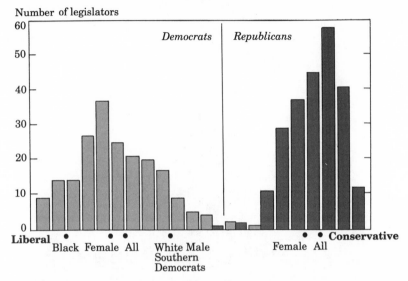

NOTE: The height of each bar shows the number of representatives with liberal-conservative positions in the range of the bar. The dots indicate the average positions of groups of representatives.
SOURCE: Authors.

FIGURE 2–6
DISTRIBUTION OF ROLL-CALL MIDPOINTS IN THE 104TH HOUSE OF REPRESENTATIVES, 1995

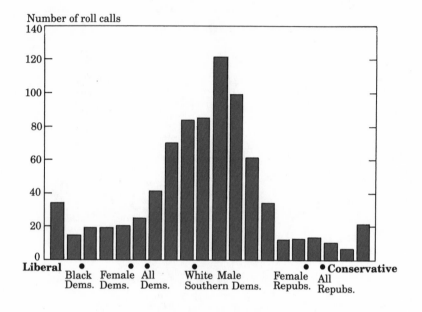

NOTE: The height of each bar shows the number of roll-call midpoints with liberal-conservative ideological position in the range of the bar. For each roll call, the midpoint is the point that best differentiates representatives who support the liberal side of the vote and those who support the conservative side. For reference, the dots indicate the average positions of groups of representatives as in figure 2–5.

SOURCE: Authors.

FIGURE 2–7
HISTOGRAM OF TWENTY-THREE REPUBLICAN SUPPORTERS OF THE
MINIMUM WAGE IN THE 104TH HOUSE OF REPRESENTATIVES,
APRIL 1996

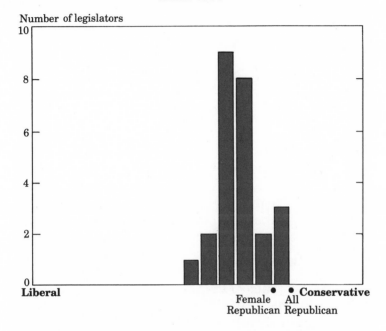

NOTE: The height of each bar shows the number of representatives with liberal-conservative positions in the range of the bar. The arrows point to the average positions of groups of representatives.
SOURCE: Authors.

3

Polarization

The distribution of legislator ideal points for the 104th House in figures 2–5, 2–6, and 2–7 shows that there is virtually no overlap in the ideological positions of the two parties. Only three Democrats— Tauzin of Louisiana, Hall of Texas, and Parker of Mississippi—are to the right of the left-most Republican, and two of these three have switched to the Republican Party (Tauzin and Parker).

This separation of the two parties continues a trend begun in the mid-1970s (Poole and Rosenthal 1984; 1997, chap. 4). Figures 3–1 and 3–2 show how far apart the members of the two parties are and how tightly dispersed the members of the two parties are around their respective party means for the post–World War II period. To measure how far apart the members of the parties are, we compute the average distance (using the coordinates from the two-dimensional linear DW-NOMINATE estimation) between all pairs of members of opposite parties. To measure the dispersion of the parties, we compute the average distance between all pairs of members of the same party. In both the House and the Senate, the average distance between members of the two parties is increasing, while the two parties are becoming increasingly homogeneous. The 1994 elections mark a continuation of a twenty-five year trend, not a unique departure.

FIGURE 3–1

AVERAGE WITHIN-PARTY AND BETWEEN-PARTY IDEOLOGICAL
DISTANCES FOR THE HOUSE OF REPRESENTATIVES, 1947–1995

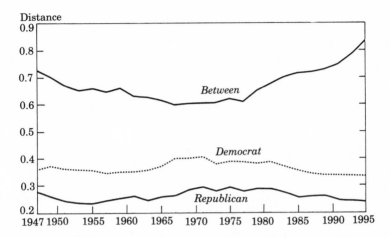

NOTE: "Between" shows the average ideological distance between
Democratic and Republican representatives, the average being
computed between all possible pairs of one Democrat and one Republican. "Democrat" shows the average ideological distance between Democrats, the average being computed over all possible
pairs of Democrats. "Republican" shows the corresponding distance for Republican pairs.
SOURCE: Computations based on DW-NOMINATE scores computed by authors.

FIGURE 3–2
AVERAGE WITHIN-PARTY AND BETWEEN-PARTY IDEOLOGICAL DISTANCES FOR THE SENATE, 1947–1995

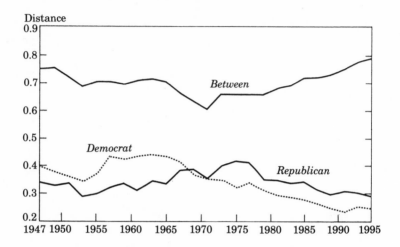

NOTE: "Between" shows the average ideological distance between Democratic and Republican senators, the average being computed between all possible pairs of one Democrat and one Republican. "Democrat" shows the average ideological distance between Democrats, the average being computed over all possible pairs of Democrats. "Republican" shows the corresponding distance for Republican pairs.

SOURCE: Computations based on DW-NOMINATE scores computed by authors.

4

Voter Identification—Two Competitive Camps

S ince the end of World War II, the grip of the two political parties on the electorate has weakened. Beginning in the mid-1960s, the number of self-proclaimed independents in the NES (National Election Study) and Gallup surveys increased dramatically.[3] As shown in figure 4–1, however, when "independents" who admit to leaning to one of the political parties are grouped with full identifiers, the picture is one of remarkable stability.[4] In the first NES survey, carried out in 1952, some 94 percent of the respondents identified with the two major parties. In 1992, this figure stood at just over 89 percent. Over the forty-year time span, Democrats lost about 10 percent of the electorate, while Republicans gained about 5 percent.

This general stability masks a dramatic change in the American South (the Confederacy plus Kentucky and Oklahoma). Figure 4–2 shows the North-South partisan splits in identification. Party identification has barely budged in the North. The Republican share in the North started at 40 percent in 1952 and finished there in 1992, with very little variation in between. In contrast, the Re-

17

FIGURE 4–1

PERCENTAGE OF VOTERS IDENTIFYING THEMSELVES AS
DEMOCRATS, AS REPUBLICANS, OR AS INDEPENDENTS LEANING
TOWARD A MAJOR PARTY, 1952–1992

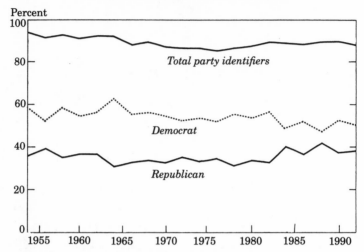

NOTE: Total party identifiers include Democrats, Republicans, and Independents who lean toward one or the other major party.
SOURCE: Authors' computations based on NES surveys.

publicans gained 16 percent of the electorate in the South. Republican gains within the South coupled with the South's greater demographic weight in the nation explain nearly all the national gains by the Republicans.

FIGURE 4–2

PERCENTAGE OF VOTERS IDENTIFYING THEMSELVES AS
DEMOCRATS, AS REPUBLICANS, OR AS INDEPENDENTS LEANING
TOWARD A MAJOR PARTY, BY REGION, 1952–1992

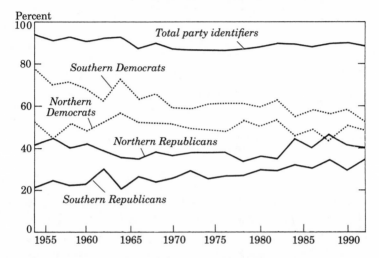

NOTE: Total party identifiers includes Democrats, Republicans, and Independents who lean toward one or the other major party.
SOURCE: Authors' computations based on NES surveys.

5

The Rich-Poor Partisan Division

P arty identification has become more linked to income (see table 5–1). Even though nationally the Democrats had lost ground to the Republicans between 1972 and 1992, they increased their edge among the poorest one-fifth of the respondents to the NES survey. At the same time, the Republican edge in the richest quintile increased.[5]

This increased separation of the rich and the poor into the two parties is not the consequence of new voters sorting on the basis of income. Table 5–2 shows effects similar to table 5–1 as we track the cohort born between 1927 and 1952. In 1972, the Democrats enjoyed some advantage in every quintile for this cohort. By 1992, the Republicans were easily ahead among the rich, while the Democrats increased their edge among the poor. It is also the case that southerners are on the whole similar to northerners in this respect. Even among white southerners, Democrats enjoy a substantial edge among the poor, and Republicans win the rich. On the whole, though, white southerners are more Republican than the nation (compare table 5–1 and table 5–3).

TABLE 5–1
PARTISAN IDENTIFICATION FOR ALL RESPONDENTS TO SURVEY, BY INCOME QUINTILE, 1972 AND 1992
(percent)

Income Quintile	1972				1992			
	D	I	R	Difference, Dem.-Rep.[a]	D	I	R	Difference, Dem.-Rep.[a]
Lowest	59	10	31	28	58	15	27	31
Second	55	16	29	26	57	11	31	26
Third	53	17	31	22	52	13	35	17
Fourth	52	10	38	14	47	8	45	2
Highest	43	12	46	−3	38	10	53	−15
Number of respondents	1,344	331	891		1,132	257	860	

NOTE: Percentages may not total 100 because of rounding.
a. Difference between Democrat and Republican.
SOURCE: NES surveys.

TABLE 5–2
PARTISAN IDENTIFICATION BY INCOME QUINTILE FOR RESPONDENTS BORN 1927–1952
(percent)

Income Quintile	1972 (Respondents Aged 20–45)				1992 (Respondents Aged 40–65)			
	D	I	R	Difference, Dem.-Rep.[a]	D	I	R	Difference, Dem.-Rep.[a]
Lowest	54	20	26	28	66	13	21	45
Second	47	21	31	16	57	13	30	27
Third	54	16	30	24	55	10	36	19
Fourth	53	13	34	19	46	10	45	1
Highest	45	14	41	4	40	8	53	−13
Number of respondents	667	220	426		434	89	304	

NOTE: Percentages may not total 100 because of rounding.
a. Difference between Democrat and Republican.
SOURCE: NES surveys.

TABLE 5-3
PARTISAN IDENTIFICATION OF WHITE SOUTHERNERS, BY INCOME QUINTILE, 1972 AND 1992
(percent)

Income Quintile	1972				1992			
	D	I	R	Difference, Dem.-Rep.[a]	D	I	R	Difference, Dem.-Rep.[a]
Lowest	55	16	30	25	51	24	25	35
Second	61	12	27	34	47	11	42	5
Third	57	16	26	31	54	11	35	19
Fourth	57	16	28	29	36	11	53	−17
Highest	48	9	43	5	32	13	55	−13
Number of respondents	341	84	189		217	70	210	

NOTE: Percentages may not total 100 because of rounding.
a. Difference between Democrat and Republican.
SOURCE: NES surveys.

6

Race and Gender

Race and gender are two issue areas with the potential of disturbing the unidimensional, polarized picture we have been painting. Figures 2–5, 2–6, and 2–7 show that these issues are likely to be strongly correlated with liberal-conservative issues. African-American Democrats anchor the left end of the dimension in the House. Within each party, female members are more liberal than male. Because, as figure 2–1 showed, almost all roll-call voting can be accounted for by a single dimension, race and gender issues do not lead to additional dimensions. But figures 2–5, 2–6, and 2–7 suggest that they may contribute to polarization of the liberal-conservative dimension.

To examine in more detail how race, gender, and, in the next chapter, income influence roll-call voting, we employ multiple regression analysis, with the results appearing in table 6–1. The dependent variable is always the DW-NOMINATE first-dimension score of the representative for either the 93rd (1973–1974), the 98th (1983–1984), or the 104th Congress (1995). The range of the score is −1.0 to +1.0. In general, the more negative the score, the more liberal the representative. The independent variables are an individual political characteristic, party, individual personal characteristics, including race and gender, and district characteristics, such as median income.

An initial observation is that we are better able to explain the DW-NOMINATE scores today than two decades ago. The R^2 is higher, and the standard error of the regression is lower. Much of this ability is due to, as previously noted, the increased separation of the parties. The difference in the party dummies changes from .097 in the 93rd House to .229 in the 98th and .481 in the 104th. In contrast, the coefficient on the South drops, consistent with our view that southern politics has become part of national politics.

The results for personal characteristics are somewhat surprising: race and Hispanic identity matter, but gender does not (there were too few Hispanics in the 93rd and 98th Houses to estimate an effect for being Hispanic so we show results only for the 104th). The gender of the representative is not statistically significant in any of the specifications shown in table 6–1, even though, as expected, the signs are all negative. Gender is a fairly weak force. The liberal voting of female members is largely a reflection of their disproportionate election from districts that would elect liberals of either gender. The districts of Shirley Chisholm, Barbara Jordan, Barbara Boxer, and Nancy Pelosi speak to this point.

In contrast, race is a big force independent of party, income, and region. To explore the effect of race better, we performed separate regressions for the North and the South (there were only two African-Americans from the South in the 93rd House and only one from the South in the 98th House, so we show results only for the 104th). Southern African-American representatives are more liberal relative to their districts than northerners. The fact that the coefficient on the percentage of African-Americans in the district is insignificant for the South may be because African-American representatives from the South are elected from districts that are mostly

TABLE 6–1
LIBERAL-CONSERVATIVE DIMENSION IN THE HOUSE OF REPRESENTATIVES, 93RD–104TH CONGRESS
(dependent variable: 1st dimension DW-NOMINATE)

Coefficient	93rd House	98th House	104th House, All	104th House, North	104th House, South
Democrat	0.194 (0.077)	−0.052 (0.067)	−0.065 (0.046)	−0.186 (0.055)	−0.016 (0.080)
Republican	0.291 (0.077)	0.177 (0.068)	0.416 (0.037)	0.464 (0.046)	0.409 (0.059)
Democrat*median Income of district	−0.015 (0.002)	−0.007 (0.002)	−0.007 (0.001)	−0.004 (0.0016)	−0.006 (0.003)
Republican*median Income of district	−0.003 (0.002)	0.004 (0.001)	−0.0006 (0.001)	−0.0016 (0.0013)	0.0008 (0.0019)
South	0.234 (0.027)	0.207 (0.020)	0.088 (0.015)	—	—
Percent African-American	−0.002 (0.001)	−0.003 (0.0008)	−0.003 (0.0008)	−0.003 (0.001)	−0.00015 (0.001)

African-American representative	−0.315 (0.073)	−0.235 (0.054)	−0.166 (0.043)	−0.073 (0.060)	−0.304 (0.060)
Percent Hispanic	—	—	−0.0003 (0.0007)	—	—
Hispanic representative	—	—	−0.144 (0.050)	—	—
Democrat*female	−0.005 (0.054)	0.023 (0.047)	−0.038 (0.027)	−0.041 (0.033)	−0.019 (0.048)
Republican*female	−0.034 (0.137)	−0.063 (0.057)	−0.034 (0.034)	−0.041 (0.039)	−0.058 (0.069)
Number of observations	434[a]	434[a]	435	298	137
Standard error of regression	0.192	0.162	0.133	0.141	0.117
Adjusted R^2	0.666	0.793	0.887	0.880	0.895

— = not used in equation.
NOTES: See appendix B for information about the independent variables. Standard errors are in parentheses.
a. The Speaker of the House did not vote enough times to receive a DW-NOMINATE score.
SOURCE: Authors' computations.

African-American. In any event, race as a personal characteristic has a big effect on how liberal the representative is. These results support our view (Poole and Romer 1993; Poole and Rosenthal 1997) that legislators have a great deal of latitude in adopting an ideological position. In other words, constituency characteristics only imperfectly predict the voting record of the representative.

African-Americans, however, are likely to represent poor districts with large African-American populations. Particularly in the North, the percentage of the district that is African-American leads to a more liberal voting record, even controlling for the race of the representative. The extreme liberal positions of African-American members is on the whole consistent with the interests of their districts. Since income is heavily correlated with race, the position of African-Americans on the liberal-conservative scale is further evidence of political polarization's relationship to income.

Hispanic as a personal characteristic has almost as big an effect on how liberal the representative is as does African-American. Similar to southern African-American representatives, however, Hispanic representatives are likely to represent poor districts with large Hispanic populations. Consequently, the percentage of the district that is Hispanic has no statistically significant effect after the personal characteristics are taken into account.

7

Income and Representation

Republicans represent districts with higher median incomes than Democrats. Expressed in 1990 dollars, the difference between the average median incomes was $3,517, $2,605, and $4,007 in the 93rd, 98th, and 104th Houses, respectively. These differences are all statistically significant.[6] Note, however, that these figures will fluctuate with seat shifts between the parties. For example, there were 174 Republican and 200 Democratic seats that did not change parties between the 103rd and 104th Houses. The average median incomes of these unchanged districts were $33,575 and $28,495, respectively, for a difference of $5,080. The average median income of the 56 seats that switched from Democrat to Republican was $29,493, which is closer to the Democratic average, thus reducing the gap between the parties in the 104th relative to the 103rd. It is interesting that the marginal districts, those lost by the Democrats, had higher median incomes than those retained.[7]

Table 6–1 shows that, controlling for race and party, income has an unexpectedly liberal effect, which is statistically significant for the Democrats but not for the Republicans. In other words, for Democrats, the richer the district, *ceteris paribus,* the more liberal the representative. This "Henry Waxman" or "limousine liberal" effect persists even after controlling for urbanization and religion (results not shown).[8] Consistent with our basic notion of politics as increasingly defined by income, however, "limousine liberalism" now has an attenuated effect. In the 93rd House, a $1,000 increase (in 1990 dollars) in the median income of a Democratic district would move that district .015 units to the left. In the 98th House, this was reduced to .007 units, and by the 104th it was down to just under .007 units—less than one half the effect twenty years earlier, although still statistically significant.

8
Presidential Voting

L ike party identification at the individual level, voting in presidential elections appears to have become more closely linked to the median income of congressional districts. Table 8–1 presents regressions of the Democratic vote for president in the Nixon-McGovern race of 1972, the Reagan-Mondale race of 1984, and the most recent two-candidate election, the Bush-Dukakis race of 1988. The Bush-Clinton-Perot race of 1992 is shown in table 8–2. Although Dukakis got over 8 percent more votes than McGovern, the cross-sectional standard deviations of the Democratic vote are very similar for the four samples (11.9, 11.9, 12.2, and 12.3, respectively). The standard errors of the regressions for our specifications for the Democratic candidates are also very similar.

The major difference in the regressions for the three two-candidate elections is that the coefficient of income is highly significant in 1984 and 1988, while it is insignificant in 1972. The magnitude of the income effect increases from 1972 to 1988, but in the three-candidate election of 1992 the effect is still statistically significant but somewhat muted. The coefficient for the South is roughly the same magnitude in the three two-candidate elections with the penalty being somewhat less for Clinton in 1992. The coefficient on the percentage of African-

TABLE 8–1

THE RELATIONSHIP OF INCOME, DISTRICT REPRESENTATION, REGION, AND RACE TO VOTING IN PRESIDENTIAL ELECTIONS FOR CONGRESSIONAL DISTRICTS, 1972, 1984, AND 1988

Coefficients	Dependent Variables		
	1972 McGovern vote in district[a]	1984 Mondale vote in district[b]	1988 Dukakis vote in district[c]
Constant	37.536	44.761	54.021
	(2.164)	(2.045)	(1.552)
Median income of district	−0.069	−0.263	−0.366
	(0.063)	(0.058)	(0.041)
1st dimension DW-NOMINATE* Democrat	−23.180	−18.682	−26.714
	(1.794)	(2.035)	(2.427)
1st dimension DW-NOMINATE* Republican	−10.189	−12.081	−6.255
	(2.160)	(2.088)	(1.945)
2nd dimension DW-NOMINATE* North	−1.220	−2.757	−3.393
	(0.999)	(0.948)	(0.778)
2nd dimension DW-NOMINATE* South	−1.178	−2.205	1.323
	(1.905)	(1.707)	(1.261)
South	−9.811	−5.631	−8.138
	(1.101)	(0.973)	(0.751)
Percent African-American	0.322	0.411	0.220
	(0.027)	(0.027)	(0.023)
Number of observations	434[d]	434[d]	435
Standard error of regression	6.755	6.379	5.972
Adjusted R^2	0.680	0.712	0.762

NOTE: See appendix B for information about the independent variables. Numbers in parentheses are standard errors.
a. All independent variables are for the 93rd (1973–74) House (1970 census).
b. All independent variables are for the 98th (1983–84) House (1980 census).
c. All independent variables are for the 104th (1995) House (1990 census).
d. The Speaker of the House did not vote enough times to receive a DW-NOMINATE score.
SOURCE: Authors' computations.

Americans fluctuates but is highly significant in all four elections. For 1992, the percentage of Hispanics in the district appears to have about one-third the effect of the percentage of African-Americans. The coefficients are all statistically significant and have the same signs as those for the percentage of African-Americans.

The ideological positions of the representatives are also very important. The Dukakis and Clinton votes both increased at least twenty-six points for a one-unit change in the liberal direction by a Democratic representative (that is, from 0.0 to -1.0), whereas McGovern got a twenty-three-point and Mondale an eighteen-point boost. For Republican-held districts, the similar comparisons are ten points in 1972, twelve in 1984, and six points in both 1988 and 1992.

The second dimension is far less important than the first DW-NOMINATE dimension, supporting our theme that political conflict is liberal-conservative in electoral politics as well as in congressional politics.

Table 8–2 also shows two regressions for the 1992 Perot vote. The coefficients strongly support the "Perot beat Bush" theory of the 1992 election. The coefficient on the 1988 Bush vote is positive and significant. Not only is Perot estimated to do well where Bush did well, but also he does well in districts where the representatives are ideologically conservative and have few African-American constituents. In addition, the coefficients on the South indicator variable and this variable interacted with the 1988 Bush vote (Bush88*South) suggest that Perot did poorer in the southern states in which Bush did well. All in all, these results make it hard to believe that Perot took many voters away from Clinton.

TABLE 8–2
THE RELATIONSHIP OF INCOME, DISTRICT REPRESENTATION, REGION, AND RACE TO VOTING IN THE 1992 PRESIDENTIAL ELECTION

Coefficients	Dependent Variables			
	Clinton vote in district	Bush vote in district	Perot vote in district	Perot vote in district (augmented regression)
Constant	41.771 (1.502)	34.373 (1.340)	22.993 (1.106)	17.571 (1.873)
Median income of district	−0.142 (0.040)	0.163 (0.035)	−0.016 (0.029)	−0.043 (0.031)
1st dimension DW-NOMINATE* Democrat	−23.080 (2.388)	20.047 (2.130)	2.875 (1.758)	4.423 (1.671)
1st dimension DW-NOMINATE* Republican	−6.091 (1.865)	4.663 (1.663)	1.431 (1.373)	—
2nd dimension DW-NOMINATE* North	−3.227 (0.747)	1.502 (0.666)	1.627 (0.549)	0.241 (0.559)
2nd dimension DW-NOMINATE* South	−0.750 (1.210)	0.580 (1.077)	0.238 (0.889)	—

	(1)	(2)	(3)	(4)
South	3.506	−2.999	7.436	−4.099
	(2.487)	(0.531)	(0.643)	(0.720)
Percent African-American	−0.165	−0.197	−0.146	0.341
	(0.019)	(0.017)	(0.020)	(0.023)
Percent Hispanic	−0.041	−0.049	−0.061	0.111
	(0.015)	(0.015)	(0.017)	(0.020)
South*Republican	0.297			
	(1.255)			
African-American* Republican	−0.136			
	(0.051)			
Bush88*Democrat	0.128			
	(0.037)			
Bush88*Republican	0.094			
	(0.037)			
Bush88*South	−0.123			
	(0.049)			
Number of observations	435	435	435	435
Standard error of regression	4.073	4.261	5.102	5.718
Adjusted R²	0.541	0.499	0.705	0.783

NOTE: See appendix B for information about the independent variables. Numbers in parentheses are standard errors.

a. All independent variables are for the 104th (1995) House (1990 Census).

SOURCE: Authors' computations.

9

The South

All the changes we outlined above lead back to the disappearance of the old Democratic Solid South. We already saw this with respect to party identification. The change in the South in presidential voting had already occurred by 1972, as the regressions in table 8–1 show. Figure 9–1 shows that this process began with the Goldwater candidacy of 1964. With the exception of the two Carter elections of 1976 and 1980, since 1964 the Republican share of the two-party vote in the South has been larger than its share in the North. Bill Clinton ran poorly in the South, even though, like Jimmy Carter, he was a southern governor. Nominating southerners may no longer prove to be an attractive strategy for Democrats.

Congressional voting was much slower to follow. White southerners had a strong incentive to maintain their influence on committees in the majority party. As figures 9–2 and 9–3 show, by 1972 the Republicans had gained strength in the South but held only 30 percent of southern seats in the House and Senate, respectively. By 1995, Republicans had won, for the first time, a majority of the southern seats in both chambers. A corollary to this gain is shown in figure 9–4. The House delegations of the two parties now have identical North-South representa-

FIGURE 9–1
REPUBLICAN PERCENTAGE OF THE TWO-PARTY VOTE FOR PRESIDENT, BY REGION, 1948–1992

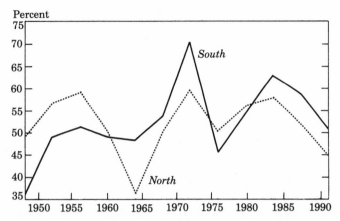

SOURCE: Authors' computations based on data from Congressional Quarterly, *Guide to U.S. Elections.*

tion. As the identification data and presidential voting regressions showed, however, the South is, everything else equal, more conservative than the remainder of the country. As a result, further Republican congressional gains can be expected in the South.

Figure 9–5 shows voting at the gubernatorial level. It lags behind the Republican presidential gains but slightly leads the gains in the House of Representatives. The graph shows the Republican percentage of the two-party vote aggregated across all states in each region.[9] There is no discernible trend in the North: Republicans have basically been competitive since the end of World War II. In the South, the realignment is clear. The Republican vote jumps sharply in the latter part of the 1960s and early 1970s and then sinks dramatically after Watergate. It then recovered in the 1980s, hitting 50 percent in the 1984 elections, and was even with or above the northern vote by 1986.

FIGURE 9–2

PERCENTAGE OF REPUBLICAN SEATS IN THE HOUSE OF
REPRESENTATIVES, BY REGION, 1946–1994

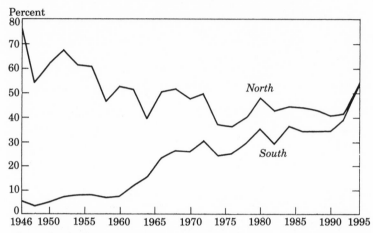

SOURCE: Authors' computations based on data from *The Historical Atlas of Political Parties in the United States Congress* and *Almanac of American Politics.*

Finally, figure 9–6 shows voting at the state legislative level. Although voting here clearly lags behind the other levels, the trends are basically the same. Republicans began gaining in the late 1960s with a fall-off after Watergate and a resumption of gains through the 1980s and early 1990s. The 1994 elections, though dramatic, were clearly a continuation of a trend toward the Republican Party in southern state legislatures. If the presidential, gubernatorial, and congressional results are any guide, and we think they are, these gains will continue until the Republicans are the majority party in the southern state legislatures.

FIGURE 9–3
PERCENTAGE OF REPUBLICAN SEATS IN THE SENATE, BY REGION, 1946–1994

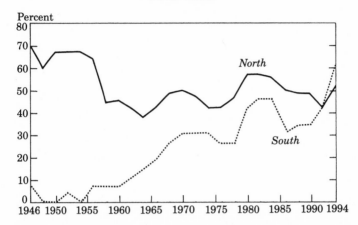

SOURCE: Authors' computations based on data from *The Historical Atlas of Political Parties in the United States Congress* and *Almanac of American Politics.*

FIGURE 9–4
PERCENTAGE OF DEMOCRATS AND REPUBLICANS FROM THE SOUTH IN THE HOUSE OF REPRESENTATIVES, 1946–1994

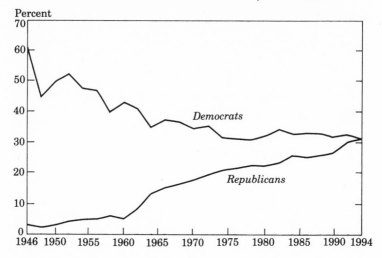

SOURCE: Authors' computations based on data from *The Historical Atlas of Political Parties in the United States Congress* and *Almanac of American Politics.*

FIGURE 9–5
REPUBLICAN PERCENTAGE OF TWO-PARTY VOTE IN GUBERNATORIAL ELECTIONS, BY REGION, 1946–1994

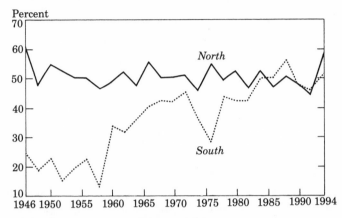

SOURCE: Authors' computations based on data from Congressional Quarterly, *Guide to U.S. Elections.*

FIGURE 9–6
REPUBLICAN PERCENTAGE OF SEATS IN UPPER AND LOWER HOUSES OF STATE LEGISLATURES, BY REGION, 1946–1994

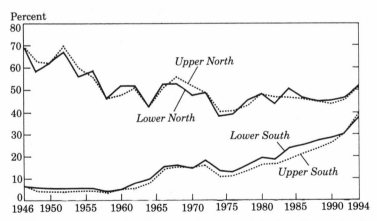

SOURCE: Authors' computations based on *Book of the States,* 1947–1993; data on the website of the National Conference of State Legislatures.

10

From Goldwater to Gingrich

The political party system of the 1940s and 1950s emerged during the latter part of the New Deal when, in the wake of the 1936 elections, northern Democrats heavily outnumbered southern Democrats in Congress. Many of the programs initiated during the subsequent Second New Deal were not to the liking of the South. Voting on minimum wages in 1937 and 1938, followed by voting during World War II on the poll tax and voting rights in the armed forces, helped to split the Democratic Party into two distinct regional wings (see Poole and Rosenthal 1997, chap. 5). Voting in Congress became two dimensional as northerners and southerners became differentiated on civil rights and related votes.

For almost thirty-five years, the United States had a three-party political system. In Congress, all three parties easily formed coalitions with one of the others against the third, depending on the issue at hand. The northern and southern Democrats united to organize the House and Senate and thereby seize the spoils due the "majority" party. The northern Democrats and Republicans united to pass the 1964 Civil Rights Act and the 1965 Voting Rights Act. And the "conservative coalition" of Republicans and southern Democrats united to block liberal economic (and, in the 1970s, social) policies.

The demise of this system began with the assassination of President Kennedy. President Johnson was able to do what Kennedy was unable to do—push fundamental civil rights legislation through Congress. This achievement was followed by President Johnson's 1964 landslide victory over an "extremist" Barry Goldwater, which produced a liberal northern Democratic congressional majority for the first time since 1936. This 89th Congress is the source of many of the expensive, redistributive programs that are so much a part of our current political debate.

We speculate that these programs along with other redistributive programs initiated by the federal courts— mandatory school busing being the most conspicuous— led to a polarizing backlash in the late 1960s and early 1970s and that the effects of this backlash were blunted by Watergate.[10] The Republican Party did not fully recover its footing until the 1980 elections.

The old southern Democratic Party has, in effect, disintegrated. White southern Democrats have been replaced by white Republicans and African-American Democrats. This trend shows little sign of slowing. During 1995, five white southern Democrats in the House— Laughlin of Texas, Parker of Mississippi, Hayes of Louisiana, Deal of Georgia, and Tauzin of Louisiana— switched to the Republican Party. In addition, sixteen white southern Democrats did not choose to run for reelection in 1996. Republicans took several of these seats.

In lockstep with the disintegration of the old southern Democratic Party is the disappearance of the second dimension of congressional voting. Race has been drawn into the first dimension because race-related issues have become increasingly redistributional—welfare, food stamps, affirmative action, and so on. It was only a matter of time before white southerners switched to the Republican Party at the congressional and local levels.

Polarization in Congress is approaching degrees not seen since the 1890s. Race and redistribution have merged into one voting dimension in Congress, and the polarization on both has sharply increased.

Where will all this change lead? The realignment of the South has greatly benefited the Republican Party. In the future, however, the Democrats may benefit from the increasing demographic weight of Hispanics in the population. Even if the Republican Party manages to become the majority party in America and takes control of Congress and the presidency, the programmatic changes in the aggregate will not be as drastic as many believe. Somehow the means will be found for the middle class to keep its Medicare and social security, or the Republicans will not be a majority party for very long. As for the poor, ending the entitlement status of welfare and Medicaid and sending the programs back to the states will not make the underlying problems disappear. The states will be unable and unwilling to end the programs altogether, and we are dubious that total government spending (federal, state, and local) will decline significantly.

DW-NOMINATE

In this appendix, we outline the DW-NOMINATE (dynamic, weighted, nominal three-step estimation) procedure we use to estimate a simple spatial model of congressional roll-call voting. A more detailed motivation of our spatial model can be found in Poole and Rosenthal (1997, chaps. 1–4).

For readers familiar with our work, DW-NOMINATE is a dynamic version of W-NOMINATE (Poole and Rosenthal, 1997, appendix A). It is very similar to our earlier D-NOMINATE procedure (Poole and Rosenthal 1991). The only differences are that DW-NOMINATE is based on normally distributed errors rather than on logit errors and that each dimension has a distinct (salience) weight. When we began our research in 1982, computer memory and speeds were a significant problem, and we took the logit approach because it was computationally more tractable. We continued to use logit in our supercomputer work (1986–1989) on D-NOMINATE. We make the change now because computer memory and speed are minor impediments and the use of the normal distribution allows us to develop much more sophisticated models of correlated error. That work is currently underway.

Below, we briefly describe DW-NOMINATE and report basic measures of fit along with a comparison to our D-NOMINATE results for the 1947–1985 period. Since the estimation procedure (except for the differences just noted) is the same as D-NOMINATE, we refer the interested reader to Poole and Rosenthal (1991, 1997), which contain very detailed descriptions of D-NOMINATE and W-NOMINATE.

The Formal Model

Let T be the number of Congresses indexed by $t = 1,...,T$; s denote the number of policy dimensions ($k = 1,...,s$); p_t denote the number of legislators in Congress t ($i = 1,...,p_t$); q_t denote the number of roll-call votes in Congress t ($j = 1,...,q_t$); and T_i denote the number of Congresses in which legislator i served ($t = 1,...,T_i$). Legislator i's coordinate on dimension k at time t is given by

$$x_{ikt} = x_{ik0} + x_{ik1}t + x_{ik2}t^2 + ... + x_{ikr}t^v, \quad (A–1)$$

where v is the degree of the polynomial.

We will confine ourselves to estimating a constant ($v = 0$) and linear ($v = 1$) model because in Poole and Rosenthal (1991) we found that higher-order models, $v = 2$ and $v = 3$, added little explanatory power.

The two roll-call outcome points can be written in terms of their midpoint and the distance between them; namely,

$$z_{jkyt} = z_{mjkt} - \delta_{jkt} \text{ and } z_{jknt} = z_{mjkt} + \delta_{jkt},$$

where, for a yea vote, z_{jkyt} is the jth outcome coordinate on the kth dimension in Congress t. Similarly, z_{jknt} is the outcome coordinate for a nay vote. The midpoint is simply

$$z_{mjkt} = (z_{jkyt} + z_{jknt})/2,$$

and δ_{jkt} is *half* the "distance" between yea and nay points on the kth dimension (note that δ_{jkt} can be negative); that is,

$$\delta_{jkt} = (z_{jkyt} - z_{jknt})/2.$$

The outcome actually chosen by legislator i will be denoted as z_{jktc} and the corresponding outcome not chosen by legislator i by z_{jktb}. This notation will greatly simplify our presentation below.

The distance of legislator i to his chosen outcome, c, on roll call j at time t is

$$d^2_{ijktc} = \sum_{k=1}^{s} (\mathbf{x}_{ikt} - z_{jktc})^2.$$

Legislator i's utility for his chosen outcome, c, on roll-call j at time, t, is

$$U_{ijtc} = u_{ijtc} + \varepsilon_{ijtc} = \beta \, exp\left[- \sum_{k=1}^{s} w_k^2 d^2_{ijktc} \right] + \varepsilon_{ijtc}, \quad \text{(A–2)}$$

where u_{ijtc} is the deterministic portion of the utility function and ε_{ijtc} is the stochastic portion. The parameter β is a signal-to-noise parameter. It determines the maximum height of the deterministic portion of the utility function. Since the stochastic portion is normally distributed with constant variance, β "adjusts" for the overall noise level. For example, if the choices by the legislators are close to random, β will be very small; if the choices by the legislators are almost exclusively a product of their positions in the policy space, β will be very large.

The probability that legislator i votes for his chosen outcome, c, is

$$P(U_{itjc} > U_{ijtb}) = P(\varepsilon_{ijtb} - \varepsilon_{ijtc} < u_{ijtc} - u_{ijtb}).$$

We make the standard assumption that the stochastic portion of the utility function is normally distributed with zero mean and variance of one-half so that the difference between two errors has a standard normal distribution; that is,

$$\varepsilon_{ijtb} - \varepsilon_{ijtc} \sim N(0, 1).$$

TABLE A–1

CLASSIFICATION PERCENTAGES, PROPORTIONAL REDUCTION IN ERRORS, AND GEOMETRIC MEAN PROBABILITIES
FOR DW-NOMINATE, HOUSE OF REPRESENTATIVES, 1947–1995

	One Dimension				Two Dimensions			
	Parameters	Percent[a]	APRE[b]	GMP[c]	Parameters	Percent[a]	APRE[b]	GMP[c]
Constant ($v = 0$)	29,228	84.5	.495	.710	58,453	86.0	.544	.729
Linear ($v = 1$)	30,219	84.7	.502	.713	60,435	86.3	.554	.733
Total number of choices	5,345,129							
Total representatives all Houses	10,974							
Number of scalable roll calls	13,505							
Number of unique representatives	2,215							

a. Percentage correctly classified.
b. Aggregate proportional-reduction-in-error (with respect to marginals).
c. Geometric mean probability.
SOURCE: Authors' computations.

Hence, the probability that legislator i votes for his chosen outcome, c, can be written in terms of the distribution function of the normal; that is,

$$P_{ijtc} = P(U_{ijtc} > U_{ijtb}) \tag{A-3}$$

$$= \Phi\{\beta(exp\left[-\sum_{k=1}^{s} w_k^2 d_{ijktc}^2\right] - exp\left[-\sum_{k=1}^{s} w_k^2 d_{ijktb}^2\right])\}.$$

If there are no missing data, then the likelihood function is

$$L = \prod_{t=1}^{T} \prod_{i=1}^{p_t} \prod_{j=1}^{q_t} P_{ijtc}. \tag{A-4}$$

To allow for missing data, let Q_t^i denote the set of roll calls for which legislator i voted at time t. (Votes include "pairs" and "announceds" as well as actual votes.) Following standard practice, we estimate parameters that maximize the log of the likelihood function. With missing data, this is

$$lnL = \sum_{t=1}^{T} \sum_{i=1}^{p_t} \sum_{j \in Q_t^i} lnP_{ijtc}. \tag{A-5}$$

For the dynamic model without missing data, let p be the number of *unique* legislators who served during the T Congresses and, for convenience, assume that every legislator serves in at least $v + 1$ Congresses with $T > v$, then the number of parameters to be estimated to maximize equation (A–5) is

$$s\sum_{t=1}^{T} 2q_t + sp(v + 1) + s + 1.$$

That is, $2sq_t$ roll-call coordinates for each Congress (the z_{mjkt} and δ_{jkt}), the $sp(v + 1)$ polynomial coefficients for the p unique legislators (the $x_{ik0}, x_{ik1}, ..., x_{ikr}$), the s dimensional (salience) weights ($w_1, w_2, ... , w_s$), and β. In actual practice, we estimate fewer than $s(v + 1)$ parameters for legislators with short periods of service.

The Estimation Algorithm. In our previous work (Poole and Rosenthal 1991, 1997), we found that there was little temporal movement in legislator positions after World War II. Consequently, we only estimate the *constant* ($v = 0$) model—legislators have the same spatial position throughout their career—and the *linear* ($v = 1$) model. We cannot use conventional methods of maximizing equation (A–5) because of the large number of parameters (see tables A–1 and A–2). Instead, we use an alternating algorithm in which the set of parameters is divided into three subsets. All the parameters are held fixed except for one subset that is estimated. Each subset of parameters is estimated in turn, while the remaining parameters are held fixed. This alternating algorithm converges to a solution in which each subset of parameters is at an optimum given that the remaining parameters are held fixed.

In our algorithm, we have three subsets of parameters—those for the legislators (the x_{ik0}, x_{ik1}, ..., x_{ikr}), those for the roll calls (the z_{mjkt} and δ_{jkt}), and the utility function (the w_k and β). In outline form, the DW-NOMINATE algorithm has three basic steps:

Step 1: Estimate the z_{mjkt} and δ_{jkt}
Step 2: Estimate the x_{ik0}, x_{ik1}, ..., x_{ikr}
Step 3: Estimate the w_k and β

Hence the acronym *D*ynamic, *W*eighted, *N*ominal *T*hree-Step *E*stimation.

Steps 1, 2, and 3 form a *global iteration*. Global iterations are repeated until the parameters in the current iteration all correlate at .99 or better with the set estimated on the previous global iteration.

We were able to implement DW-NOMINATE for the post–World War II period on Pentium personal computers with large memories (a minimum of 64 meg of RAM is required). Rather than writing one large program, we wrote separate, stand-alone programs to implement each

TABLE A-2
CLASSIFICATION PERCENTAGES, PROPORTIONAL REDUCTION IN ERRORS, AND GEOMETRIC MEAN PROBABILITIES FOR DW-NOMINATE, SENATE, 1947–1995
(percent)

	One Dimension				Two Dimensions			
	Parameters	Percent[a]	APRE[b]	GMP[c]	Parameters	Percent[a]	APRE[b]	GMP[c]
Constant ($v = 0$)	28,820	82.0	.433	.677	57,637	84.2	.504	.702
Linear ($v = 1$)	29,045	82.3	.443	.681	58,087	86.5	.513	.707
Total number of choices	1,289,703							
Total senators all Senates	2,503							
Number of scalable roll calls	13,505							
Number of unique senators	441							

a. Percentage correctly classified.
b. Aggregate proportional-reduction-in-error (with respect to marginals).
c. Geometric mean probability.
SOURCE: Authors' computations.

of the steps above. This was possible because we could use the D-NOMINATE results as *starting coordinates* for DW-NOMINATE (for the 80th through the 99th Congresses). Not surprisingly, this led to very quick convergence—only two global iterations were necessary for the House and Senate. The Pearson correlations between the coordinates from D-NOMINATE and DW-NOMINATE for the two-dimensional linear ($v = 1$) model for the House were .974 for the first dimension and .926 for the second dimension (the n was 8,787 for the 80th through the 99th Houses). The corresponding correlations for the Senate were .964 and .913 respectively (the n was 2,000 for the 80th through the 99th Senates).

For the two-dimensional estimation, we departed from our D-NOMINATE approach of estimating one dimension at a time (see Poole and Rosenthal 1997, appendix A, for details) in favor of estimating both dimensions simultaneously. We took this approach for two reasons. First, the D-NOMINATE one-dimension-at-a-time approach is very memory intensive. We had to use a supercomputer to estimate the D-NOMINATE model. Second, given the fact that the spatial model estimated by D-NOMINATE is the same as that outlined here save for the dimension (salience) weights, we were confident that the D-NOMINATE legislator coordinates would be very close to those that would be estimated by DW-NOMINATE. Consequently, performing step 1 with the two-dimensional D-NOMINATE coordinates would allow us to estimate the roll-call coordinates on both dimensions quite easily. For the 100th through the 104th Houses and Senates, we used coordinates from W-NOMINATE for starts. We retained the same constraints on the estimated coordinates that we used in D-NOMINATE; namely, the estimated legislator constant terms and roll-call midpoints are constrained to lie within a hypersphere of radius one:

TABLE A–3
PARAMETER ESTIMATES FOR HOUSE OF REPRESENTATIVES

	One Dimension		Two Dimensions	
	Estimate	Standard error	Estimate	Standard error
Constant Model (v = 0)				
β^a	3.364	5.9×10^{-6}	3.663	6.7×10^{-6}
w_2^b			.307	1.0×10^{-7}
Linear Model (v = 1)				
β^a	3.375	6.0×10^{-6}	3.677	6.8×10^{-6}
w_2^b			.305	1.0×10^{-7}

a. Signal-to-noise parameter.
b. Weight on second dimension.
SOURCE: Authors' computations.

$$\sum_{k=1}^{s} x_{ik0}^2 \le 1 \text{ and } \sum_{k=1}^{s} z_{mjkt}^2 \le 1.$$

We also constrain the salience weight of the first dimension to be equal to 1; that is, $w_1 = 1.0$. As a practical matter, there is some interaction between the salience weights—the w_k—and β. Given the constraint on the legislator and roll-call midpoints, we can set the first dimension weight equal to 1 and estimate the remaining weights on dimensions 2, 3, etc., and β will adjust to compensate.

To get standard errors for our converged parameters, we employ a variation of the standard technique of calculating the outer product matrix of the vector of partial derivatives; that is, let g be the vector of partial derivatives, then

$$\Delta = \Sigma \, gg',$$

where the sum is over the number of observations. In our problem, however, the matrix for the House of Representatives for the two-dimensional model would be approxi-

TABLE A–4
PARAMETER ESTIMATES FOR SENATE

	One Dimension		Two Dimensions	
	Estimate	Standard error	Estimate	Standard error
Constant Model (v = 0)				
β^a	3.434	.000027	3.784	.000031
w_2^b			.314	5.0×10^{-7}
Linear Model (v = 1)				
β^a	3.451	.000027	3.799	.000031
w_2^b			.312	5.0×10^{-7}

a. Signal-to-noise parameter.
b. Weight on second dimensions.
SOURCE: Authors' computations.

mately 60,000 by 60,000 (see table A–1), and it is impractical to invert a matrix of that size. Consequently, we form Δ for each of the three subsets of parameters conditional on the other parameters being held fixed. Consequently, the standard errors produced for the subsets of parameters, given that the other parameters are held fixed, must be viewed as *heuristic descriptive statistics* (see tables A–3 and A–4). Comparison of D-NOMI-NATE standard errors with those computed by bootstrap methods (Poole and Rosenthal 1991, 1997), however, suggests that these not "econometrically correct" standard errors would be close to bootstrap standard errors.

Description of Variables

African-American representative. Identification of members by Congressional Research Service Report "Black Members of the United States Congress, 1789–1989," and 1996 *Almanac of American Politics*.

Gubernatorial votes. From Congressional Quarterly's *Guide to U.S. Elections*.

Hispanic representative. From 1996 *Almanac of American Politics* and 1996 *Politics in America*.

Median income of district (thousands of 1990 dollars). Median family income reported in 1974, 1984, and 1996 *Almanacs of American Politics*. The figures are based on the 1970, 1980, and 1990 censuses, respectively.

Party composition of state legislatures. From *Book of the States*, 1947–1993; and the website of the National Conference of State Legislatures (www.ncsl.org).

Percentage African-American. Percentage of district population of African-American heritage reported in 1974, 1984, and 1996 *Almanacs of American Politics*. The figures are based on the 1970, 1980, and 1990 censuses, respectively.

Percentage Hispanic. Percentage of district population of Hispanic heritage reported in 1974, 1984, and 1996 *Almanacs of American Politics*. The figures are based on the 1970, 1980, and 1990 censuses, respectively.

Presidential votes. Percentage of presidential vote by district as reported by 1974, 1984, and 1996 *Almanacs of American Politics*.

South. Dummy variable for the representatives and districts in Alabama, Arkansas, Florida, Georgia, Kentucky, Louisiana, Mississippi, North Carolina, Oklahoma, South Carolina, Tennessee, Texas, and Virginia.

Woman representative. Identification of members in *Women in Congress, 1917–1976,* U.S. Congress Joint Committee on Arrangement for the Commemoration of the Bicentennial, and the 1996 *Almanac of American Politics*.

Notes

1. The only differences are that it is based on normally distributed errors rather than on logit errors and that each dimension has a distinct (salience) weight. The salience weights are held constant over the estimation period while legislator positions can change as linear functions of time.

2. This point is extensively documented in Poole and Rosenthal (1991, 1997) and in Poole and Romer (1993).

3. For example, see Stanley and Niemi (1994) figures 5–1 and 5–2, pp. 159–60.

4. Leaners do not behave very differently from weak partisans (Petrocik 1989).

5. The quintiles were defined by sorting the sample by income and then splitting into five subsamples of equal size. It is possible that several respondents had the same reported income, with some put in one quintile and the others in the next highest quintile. More stable estimates could be achieved by appropriate averaging techniques.

6. In the 93rd Congress, the average median income in 1990 dollars for Democrats was \$29,610 and for Republicans, \$33,127. This difference was statistically significant with one tailed p-value of .000002. In the 98th, the average median income for Democrats was \$30,534 and for Republicans, \$33,139 with a one tailed p-value of .00003. In the 104th, the average median income for Democrats was \$28,563 and for Republicans, \$32,570 with one tailed p-value of .000002. If the average income

rather than the median income of the district is used, the p-values are even smaller.

7. The difference is not statistically significant—the t-value is approximately .98.

8. An entertaining discussion of this phenomenon is Tom Wolfe's *Radical Chic and Mau-Mauing the Flak Catchers* (New York: Bantam Books, 1971).

9. That is, the Republican percentage of the two-party vote is the ratio of all votes for Republican candidates for governor to all votes for Republican and Democratic candidates for governor in all the northern and southern states.

10. The reasons for this polarization are discussed in Phillips (1969) and Scammon and Wattenberg (1970).

References

Converse, Philip E. 1964. "The Nature of Belief Systems in Mass Publics." In David E. Apter, ed., *Ideology and Discontent*. New York: Free Press.

Petrocik, John R. 1989. "An Expected Party Vote: New Data for an Old Concept." *American Journal of Political Science* 33:44–66.

Phillips, Kevin B. 1969. *The Emerging Republican Majority*. Garden City, N.Y.: Doubleday & Co., Inc.

Poole, Keith T., and Thomas Romer. 1993. "Ideology, Shirking and Representation." *Public Choice* 77: 185–96.

Poole, Keith T., and Howard Rosenthal. 1984. "The Polarization of American Politics." *Journal of Politics* 46:1061–79.

———. 1991. "Patterns of Congressional Voting." *American Journal of Political Science* 35:228–78.

———. 1997. *Congress: A Political-Economic History of Roll Call Voting*. New York: Oxford University Press (forthcoming).

Scammon, Richard M., and Ben J. Wattenberg. 1970. *The Real Majority*. New York: Coward, McCann & Geoghegan, Inc.

Stanley, Harold W., and Richard G. Niemi. 1994. *Vital Statistics on American Politics*. Washington, D.C.: CQ Press.

About the Authors

NOLAN M. MCCARTY is an assistant professor of political science at Columbia University. His research is concerned with the performance of legislative and executive institutions as well as the role of interest groups in the political process. He is currently engaged in research on the polarization of American politics and the dynamics of interest group access in Congress.

KEITH T. POOLE is professor of politics and political economy in the Graduate School of Industrial Administration, Carnegie Mellon University. His research is concerned with the history of congressional voting and economic regulation, and he is the author and coauthor of numerous articles about the U.S. Congress. His latest book, written with Howard Rosenthal, is *Congress: A Political-Economic History of Roll Call Voting,* from Oxford University Press.

HOWARD ROSENTHAL is Roger Williams Straus Professor of Social Sciences at Princeton University. His previous books include *Partisan Politics, Divided Government and the Economy* and *Prediction Analysis of Cross Classifications.* His current ambitions include integrating the history of popular elections with the history of elite behavior in legislatures.

AEI STUDIES ON UNDERSTANDING
ECONOMIC INEQUALITY
Marvin H. Kosters, series editor

THE DISTRIBUTION OF WEALTH: INCREASING INEQUALITY?
John C. Weicher

EARNINGS INEQUALITY: THE INFLUENCE OF CHANGING
OPPORTUNITIES AND CHOICES
Robert H. Haveman

INCOME MOBILITY AND THE MIDDLE CLASS
*Richard V. Burkhauser, Amy D. Crews, Mary C. Daly,
and Stephen P. Jenkins*

INCOME REDISTRIBUTION AND THE REALIGNMENT
OF AMERICAN POLITICS
Nolan M. McCarty, Keith T. Poole, and Howard Rosenthal

RELATIVE WAGE TRENDS, WOMEN'S WORK,
AND FAMILY INCOME
Chinhui Juhn

WAGE INEQUALITY: INTERNATIONAL COMPARISONS
OF ITS SOURCES
Francine D. Blau and Lawrence M. Kahn